W9-BPJ-265

MY DIARY

Created by Bernice Myers

SCHOLASTIC INC.
New York Toronto London Auckland Sydney

For Robin and Brian

ISBN 0-590-32409-8

20 1 2 3 4 5/9

Printed in the U.S.A. 40

Favorites

FOOD ______________________________

FRIEND ______________________________

TEAM ______________________________

SPORT ______________________________

MONSTER ______________________________

MOVIE ______________________________

TEACHER ______________________________

SCHOOL SUBJECT ______________________________

SNACK ______________________________

AUNT ______________________________

UNCLE ______________________________

Vital Statistics

NAME ____________________

ADDRESS ____________________

MOTHER'S NAME ____________________

FATHER'S NAME ____________________

BROTHERS' NAME ____________________

SISTERS' NAME ____________________

NICKNAME ____________________

AGE ____________________

DATE OF BIRTH ____________________

WHERE BORN ____________________

NAME OF HOSPITAL ____________________

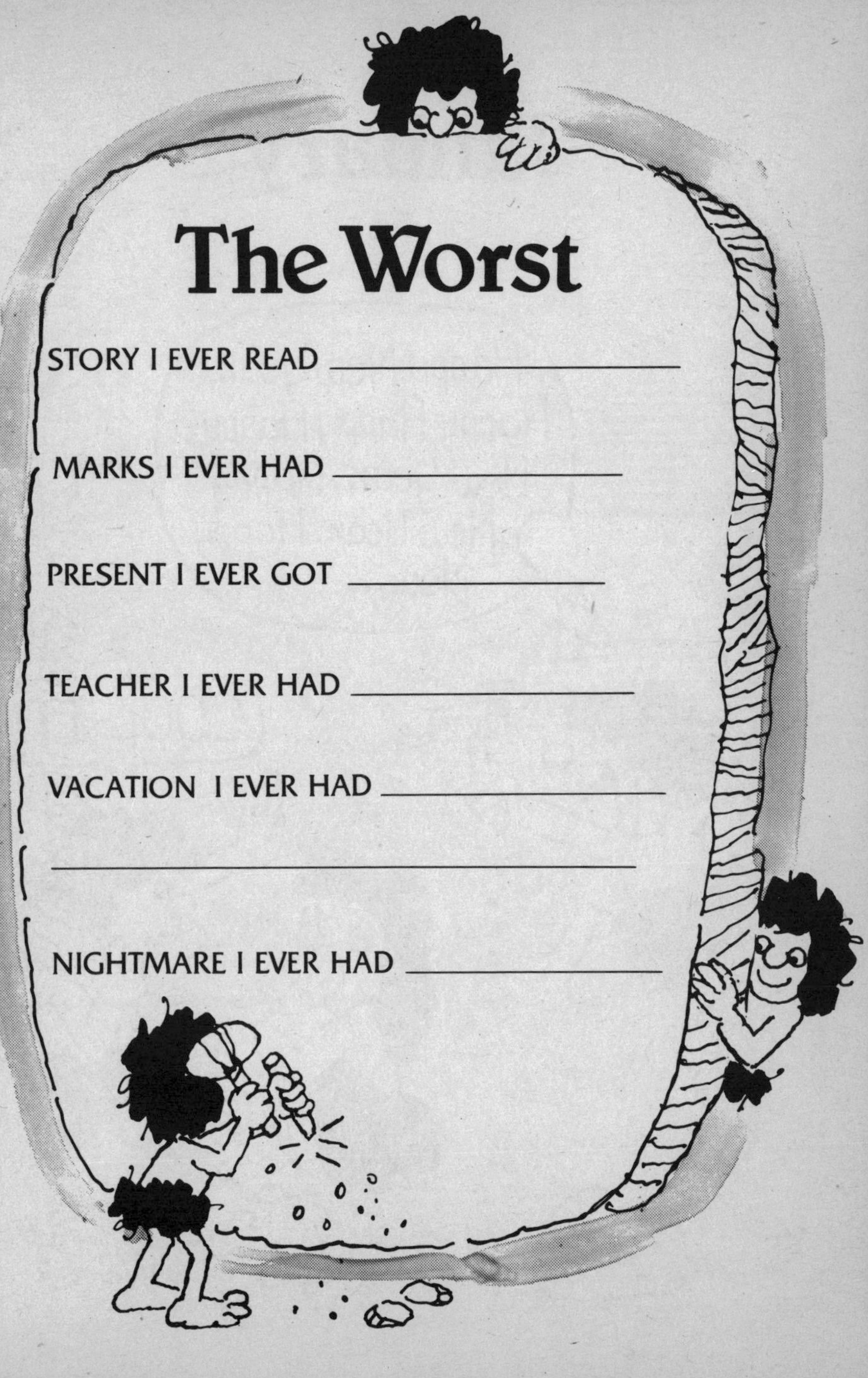

The Worst

STORY I EVER READ ____________________

MARKS I EVER HAD ____________________

PRESENT I EVER GOT ____________________

TEACHER I EVER HAD ____________________

VACATION I EVER HAD ____________________

____

NIGHTMARE I EVER HAD ____________________

January

Happy New Year.. Happy Happy Happy New Year.. Happy New Year.. Happy New...
COOL IT!

1

2

3

4

5
Jan.

6

7

8

9

10

11

Why are a calendar and a palm tree alike?

They both have dates.

12

Jan.

13

14

15

16

17

18

Which is right?
14+18 is 33...or
14+18 are 33.
Neither.
14+18 are 32.

19

Jan.

20

21

22

23

24

25

Do you
hunt bear?
If I hunted
bare, I'd
catch cold.

26

Jan.

27

28

29

30

31

Why do birds fly south in winter?
It's too far to walk.

February

What do you guys wanna' be when you grow up?

1

2

3

4

5

Feb.

6

7

8

9

10

11

Which month has 28 days?
They all have.

12
Feb.

13

14

Hey, did the school play have a happy ending?

15

16

17

Yeah! We were all glad when it was over...

18
Feb.

19

20

That's the smartest dog I ever saw!

21

22

23

He's not so smart.
I'm winning.

24

Feb.

25

26

Peep
Tweet
peep
caw

27

28

29

Hey, buy me! I'll help you do homework.

March

Spring makes me feel like a beautiful flower.
Yeah! A DAFFY-dil.

1

2

3

4

5
Mar.

6

7

8

9

10

11

What's the difference between a new penny and an old dime?

Nine cents.

12
Mar.

13

14

15

16

17

18

What's easy
to get into
but hard to
get out of.

Trouble.

19

Mar.

20

21

22

23

24

25

Mom, you don't have to worry anymore about my breaking your jar...

26

Mar.

27

28

Do you
serve
crabs
here?

29

30

31

We serve everybody...

April

They are pretty...
But they're just
too big to hide!

1

2

3

4

5

Apr.

6

7

8

9

10

11

It's raining
cats
and dogs.

I know.
I just
stepped
in a poodle.

12

Apr.

13

14

15

16

17

18

You milkin' the cow in your new hat?
'Course not. In the pail.

19

Apr.

20

21

Do you know it takes
two sheep to make
a sweater?

22

23

24

I didn't even know sheep could knit.
ZOO

25
Apr.

26

27

Where are you taking that dinosaur?
Wherever he wants to go...

28

29

30

May

...Put them all together they spell MOTHER...
MOTHA

1

2

3

4

5

May

6

7

8

9

10

11

I'm going away to study singing.
Far away, I hope!

12
May

13

14

15

16

17

18

Will the hot dogs be much longer?

No. This is the longest they get.

19

May

20

21

22

23

24

25

Sam, stop scratching yourself.
Why? Nobody else knows where I itch.

26

May

27

28

Are you
fishing, Ozzie?

29

30

31

Naw!
I'm drowning
worms:..

June

No more pencils,
No more books...

1

2

3

4

5
June

6

7

8

9

10

11

Tell the truth, June
and don't Ju-ly.

12
June

13

14

15

16

17

18

Why is
Sunday
the
strongest
day?
Because
all the
others
are
'weak'
days.

19
June

20

21

You can catch more flies with sugar than with vinegar.

22

23

24

But what will you do with all those flies?

25

June

26

27

Do you know how long cows should be milked?

28

29

30

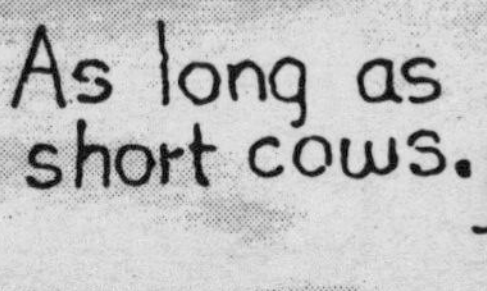
As long as
short cows.

July

But I don't want to be the first firecracker...

1

2

3

4

5

July

6

7

8

9

10

11

You tell ém, horse!
The answer is neigh.

12

July

13

14

15

16

17

18

The doctor
put me on a
7-day diet.
You look
like you
ate it all
in one meal.

19

July

20

21

22

23

24

25

What's gray,
has 4 legs
and a trunk?

A mouse
on vacation.

26
July

27

28

Hello...

29

30

31

I didn't know
an ox could
talk.
Neither
did I.

August

I wonder why August has no holidays?
...'cause it's too hot to celebrate anything...

1

2

3

4

5
Aug.

6

7

8

9

10

11

Where does
a baby dog
sleep?
In a
pup tent.

12

Aug.

13

14

15

16

17

18

Why do you put popcorn into the eggs?
So they turn themselves over.

19

Aug.

20

21

22

23

24

25

Why are a tree and a dog alike?
They both have a bark.

26

Aug.

27

28

Don't be afraid
of his bark.
His tail is
wagging.

29

30

31

But which end should I believe?

September

Only 9 more months 'til summer vacation.

1

2

3

4

5

Sept.

6

7

8

9

10

11

Why don't you take a bus?
I'd be arrested.

12

Sept.

13

14

15

16

17

18

My brother's been walking since he's 8 months old.
He must be tired.

19
Sept.

20

21

I'm punishing you
for not doing your
homework.

22

23

24

But that's punishing
me for something
I didn't do.

25

Sept.

26

27

That doesn't look like a Police dog.

28

29

30

That's 'cause
he's in
disguise.

October

Gee Ma...
Newts, frog hearts
and snake-eyes
again for supper!

1

2

3

4

5

Oct.

6

7

8

9

10

11

What's the weather like outside?

I can't see. It's too foggy.

12

Oct.

13

14

15

16

17

18

What are you gonna' do for your science project?
I'm going to shrink my brother's head.

19

Oct.

20

21

22

23

24

25

Willie's playing on the piano.
Tell him to get off and play on the floor.

26
Oct.

27

28

What are you giving Jimmy for his birthday?

29

30

31

My cold...

November

Today, I'm thankful I'm not a turkey...

1

2

3

4

5
Nov.

6

7

8

9

10

11

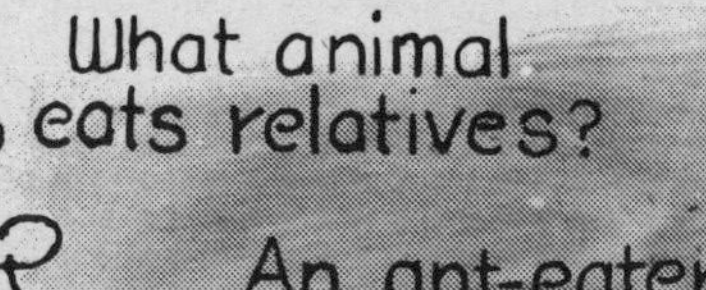
What animal
eats relatives?
An ant-eater.

12

Nov.

13

14

15

16

17

18

Don't cry like that...
Why? Is there another way to cry?

19
Nov.

20

21

Did you push Sam
down that flight
of stairs?

22

23

24

I only pushed him down one step. He fell down the other 12 himself.

25

Nov.

26

27

We can always
count on
one thing.

28

29

30

What?
Our fingers.

December

Why can't you use the front door like everyone else..?

1

2

3

4

5

Dec.

6

7

8

9

10

11

How can I
stop the
water
coming
into my
house?

Don't pay
your bill.

12
Dec.

13

14

15

16

17

18

Why does a hummingbird hum?
He probably doesn't know the words.

19
Dec.

20

21

22

23

24

25

What would happen if I threw a green stone into the Red Sea?

26

Dec.

27

28

Do you
write
better on
an empty
stomach or
a full one?

29

30

31

I write
better on
paper.

January

Happy New Year.. Happy Happy Happy New Year.. Happy New Year.. Happy New...
COOL IT!

1

2

3

4

5

Jan.

6

7

8